Java

Travel Guide

2025 - 2026

Volcanoes, Temples, and Tea Plantations —
Explore Indonesia's Heartland with Local
Secrets, Authentic Food, and Unforgettable
Adventures

Curt L. Ortiz

COPYRIGHT

TABLE OF CONTENTS

INTRODUCTION: JAVA - THE MEETING POINT OF EARTH, CULTURE, AND FLAVOR

Java is a place that eats you, not just a destination.

It's Yogyakarta's sultry nighttime air filled with the rhythmic clang of a gamelan orchestra. the earthy aroma of freshly made pulled tea, or teh tarik, in a street café in Bandung. In the pale, pre-dawn light, you can feel the crunch of volcanic gravel beneath your feet as you approach Mount Bromo's rim. In 2025–2026, Java will be more vibrant than ever. It is a living, breathing island where nature, history, and everyday life are all seamlessly intertwined together.

Java serves as a rapid transit point between Bali and Sumatra, and most visitors to Indonesia merely explore its surface. But those who stay and explore find an island that can feel like a number of countries combined into one: from remote volcanic peaks to serene coastal waters; from ancient Hindu-Buddhist temples to Islamic prayer calls resonating across city rooftops; from megacities pulsing with modern energy to villages where time seems to have stopped a century ago.

The purpose of this book is to take you far away from the usual tourist route. Without the deluge of generic, never-ending internet advice, it's about experiencing Java the way locals do.

Why Your Next Adventure Should Be in Java

Indonesia's geographical and cultural center is Java. Despite housing more than half of the country's people, its diversity in terms of landscapes and lifestyles is astounding. You may begin your day in a Jakartan skyscraper hotel, travel through verdant rice terraces on a high-speed train, and end it with ginger tea in the shade of a centuries-old temple.

The island's differences are what make it so appealing:

- **Natural Wonders:** Java is a haven for hikers, photographers, and adventurers, with everything from smoking volcanoes like Bromo and Ijen to the emerald-green slopes of the Dieng Plateau.
- **Cultural Depth:** Temples, palaces, and unique art forms have been left behind by centuries of Hindu, Buddhist, Islamic, and colonial influences.
- **Culinary Richness:** The food of Java is an adventure in and of itself, with strong flavors, fragrant spices, and a tea culture that elevates a basic beverage to a social event.
- **Warm Hospitality:** The Javanese are renowned for their gentle humor, kindness, and politeness. A straightforward "terima kasih" (thank you) can lead to unanticipated generosity.

Java is not only open for travel in 2025–2026, but it is also more accessible than before. You can travel more easily and safely thanks to high-speed rail, improved online reservation platforms, growing tourism efforts, and infrastructure upgrades. However, there are still many areas of the island where the contemporary world hasn't encroached.

How to Utilize This Manual

This handbook is not for daydreaming; it is for actual travel. Each chapter is intended to provide you with the broad overview as well as the specifics that will facilitate your journey.

You will discover:

- Specific advice on how to avoid crowds at popular destinations.
- Hidden locations that are completely ignored by most guidebooks.
- Time and cost-saving transportation tips.

- Cultural clues that convey respect and help you fit in.
- Current information for 2025–2026, including new attractions and access criteria.

After a brief introduction to establish the scene, each chapter covers five major subtopics that are brimming with useful information. Every chapter ends with a succinct conclusion that wraps everything up and offers suggestions for how to continue using those experiences throughout your journey.

New Developments for 2025–2026

Javan travel is changing. Weekend getaways are now more feasible thanks to the high-speed train line that connects Bandung and Jakarta. Islands are simpler to visit thanks to improved ferry connections to Madura and Karimunjawa. To preserve their legacy, well-known sites like Borobudur have changed tourist quotas, therefore it's now crucial to understand the reservation procedure beforehand.

Additionally, sustainable tourism is receiving more attention. More choices now allow you to enjoy Java without endangering its ecology or culture, from eco-lodges close to volcanoes to village tours led by the local population. These aren't merely "green" decisions; they're frequently the most fulfilling and genuine.

Cultural Etiquette: Respectful Travel

Java has a long history. Even if cities are diverse and modern, respecting local traditions will always make your trip more enjoyable. Here are some fundamentals to keep in mind:

- It's a good idea to cover your knees and shoulders when you visit temples or rural areas.
- It's considered more courteous to give or receive with your right hand.

- Smile a lot; being friendly is a cultural standard and is frequently reciprocated.
- Learn a few Javanese or Bahasa Indonesian language; even simple greetings might lead to real connections.

A Trip Through Temples, Teh, and Volcanoes

The subtitle of this book is more than just poetic; it serves as a road map for the moments you will cherish the most. Java's untamed, unadulterated nature is symbolized by its volcanoes. The island's historical and spiritual pillars are temples. And tea, a simple yet deep beverage, is a symbol of daily life that is enjoyed by families, friends, and strangers.

In the upcoming chapters, you'll stand on the brink of volcano craters, explore temple passageways that were chiseled out over a millennium ago, and stop at peaceful warungs, which are little local restaurants, where tea is served in glass cups with the sugar gently melting at the bottom.

Why You Will Remember This Trip

Traveling to Java is about more than just seeing the sights; it's about changing. You'll leave with more than just pictures:

- A greater understanding of how civilizations change and coexist.
- A memory of culinary flavors that you can't get anywhere else.
- Awe-inspiring scenery that makes you appreciate the size and might of nature.
- Narratives about interpersonal relationships that linger in your memory long after you've returned home.

If you take the time to look, Java gives you the unique opportunity to see a nation's soul. Additionally, this technique will ensure that you experience it rather than just see it.

Welcome to the island trip of a lifetime. Java will provide you more than you could ever ask for, whether your goals are the street food feasts, the temple sunsets, the volcanic excursions, or the peaceful moments spent sipping hot tea.

The island will reveal itself to you in ways that no map or website can adequately capture if you approach it with respect and curiosity.

Your adventure has just begun. Let's get started.

CHAPTER 1: MAKING TRAVEL PLANS TO JAVA

Every fantastic journey starts long before you board the aircraft. Java views preparation as more than simply packing your bags; it's about making the correct choices at the appropriate moment to guarantee a seamless, economical, and incredibly fulfilling trip. The island's infrastructure and tourism industry are changing quickly in 2025–2026, but so are booking systems, transportation networks, and admission regulations. From scheduling your trip to dealing with visas, scheduling transportation, and getting the best lodging, this chapter will guide you through every crucial decision so that you can arrive in Java prepared to enjoy rather than solve.

1.1 Planning Your Vacation: The Greatest Months to Go

Although Java is tropical all year round, the experience changes significantly from May to September (dry season) to October to April (wet season).

- **Dry Season (Best Overall):** Ideal for hiking volcanoes and visiting temples, this season offers clear skies, less travel disturbance, and simpler trekking. Prices are higher and there are more people during the busiest months (June to August), particularly in the vicinity of Borobudur and Bromo.

- **Wet Season:** Less tourists and lush scenery, although transportation may be hampered by intense afternoon rains. Great for photography, city exploring, and cultural activities.

- **Particular Dates to Take Into Account:**

- The magnificent Buddhist event known as the Waisak Festival takes place at Borobudur, usually in May or June.
- Travel slows down during Ramadan (dates vary each year), and some eateries close during the day, but the evening food markets come alive.
- August 17 is Independence Day; parades and celebrations are to be expected.

Advice: May and September are the best months if you want a mix of pleasant weather, less costs, and fewer tourists.

1.2 Requirements for Entry and Available Visas

In 2025, Indonesia's visa regulations were broadened to promote travel and improve entry management.

- **Visa-Free & Visa on Arrival (VoA):** Visitors from more than 90 nations are allowed entry into

Java without a visa for a maximum of 30 days, or they can purchase a 30-day VoA for about IDR 500,000 (about USD 35). At immigration offices in big cities, the VoA may be extended once more for a total of thirty days.

- **E-Visa:** Online access is advised if you wish to skip the lines at the airport. Especially helpful if you want to remain longer than 60 days.

- Requirements include documentation of further travel, a passport that is valid for at least six months, and occasionally evidence of adequate income.

- **Health Regulations:** Most visitors are not needed to get any vaccinations, but those coming from specific nations must provide documentation of their yellow fever immunization. It is highly advised to get emergency and COVID-19 travel insurance.

Pro Tip: Arriving midday or late at night usually reduces wait times at immigration, which can be lengthy during peak arrival hours in Jakarta.

1.3 Java Budgeting

Depending on your preferences, Java can be incredibly inexpensive or opulent. Here's what to anticipate in 2025:

- **Budget Travelers:** $25–40 per day, including public transportation, street food, and local guesthouses.
- Mid-Range: $50 to $100 a day; this includes guided excursions, boutique hotels, and sporadic indulgences.
- Luxurious accommodations, private drivers, fine food, and resorts cost more than $150 per day.

Breakdown of Daily Costs (Mid-Range example):

- Lodging: $30 to $50
- Drinks & Food: $15–25
- Transportation: $10–$20

- Tours and Activities: $20–40

Always have some Indonesian Rupiah (IDR) on hand, especially in rural areas where cash is still king. While they are widespread in urban areas, ATMs can be hard to find in rural areas.

1.4 Accessing Java

There are three primary international gateways for Java:

- For business travel, connecting flights, and seeing western Java, Jakarta (Soekarno-Hatta International Airport) is the best option.
- Bromo, Ijen, and East Java may all be easily reached from Surabaya (Juanda International Airport).
- The best place to visit Borobudur, Prambanan, and the cultural center of Central Java is Yogyakarta (YIA, Yogyakarta International Airport).

Advice for Flying:

- Low-cost airlines like AirAsia and Scoot frequently have promotions from Southeast Asia.
- The majority of flights from North America and Europe connect at Singapore, Kuala Lumpur, or Doha.
- There are many domestic flights in Indonesia, however they can be delayed, so allow extra time for connections.

1.5 Making Hotel Reservations

From five-star hotels to bamboo guesthouses, Java has it all.

- The best places to find foreign chains, business hotels, and rooftop bars are Jakarta and Surabaya.

- Yogyakarta: Homestays, traditional Javanese joglo houses, and charming boutique accommodations.
- Near Volcanoes: For sunrise walks, consider rustic accommodations near Bromo or Dieng Plateau.
- Farm stays and jungle retreats that help local communities are examples of eco-stays, which are becoming more and more popular.

Method of Booking:

- For stays in cities, use booking systems; however, for better rates in rural areas, get in touch with establishments directly.
- Make reservations at least two to three months in advance for significant festivals or holidays.
- Verify check-in times at all times because certain distant properties need transportation cooperation.

Useful Pre-Trip Advice

- Connectivity options include using eSIM services or purchasing a local SIM card at the airport (Telkomsel has the best coverage).

- Essentials for packing include a rain jacket, light, breathable clothing, modest temple garb, hiking shoes for volcanoes, a universal adapter, and a reusable water bottle.

- **Language:** Since Bahasa Indonesia is commonly used, it helps to learn simple greetings like "Selamat pagi" (good morning).

- **Apps to Get:**

  - Grab (ride-hailing)
  - Traveloka (booking flights and hotels)
  - The offline version of Google Translate
  - Offline maps at Maps.me

You don't start your journey to Java at the airport; rather, it starts with your planning. You'll have more time and energy for impromptu exploring once you get there if you prepare ahead of time. The most common travel anxieties can be eliminated by selecting the appropriate season, being aware of visa requirements, planning your finances carefully, and reserving lodging and transportation in advance.

The prize? More time for the good things, like strolling through the artistically decorated alleys of Yogyakarta, sipping tea while the rain patters on a bamboo roof, and watching Mount Bromo erupt in the gentle morning light.

We'll then go from preparing to experiencing, beginning in Jakarta, the bustling metropolis of the island and probably where you'll first see Java's amazing contrasts.

CHAPTER 2: JAKARTA - THE ENTRANCE TO THE VITALITY AND DIVERSITY OF JAVA

Jakarta is more than just the capital of Indonesia; it is the place where the pulse of the country is most strongly felt. Jakarta is frequently the first destination for tourists traveling to Java; it is chaotic yet alluring, modern yet rich in heritage. Many visitors view it as a brief stopover, but those who stay find a city full of vibrant neighborhoods, delicious street food, cultural treasures, and an inspiring tale of perseverance. This chapter will teach you how to take full advantage of Jakarta, from its rich history to its bustling nightlife, so that your trip to Java begins with a lively introduction rather than a quick trip to the airport.

2.1 Orientation in Jakarta

With about 11 million inhabitants in the city proper and over 30 million in the larger metropolitan region (Jabodetabek), Jakarta is a sprawling city on Java's northwest coast.

Important Districts to Be Aware of:

- Merdeka Square, the National Monument (Monas), and government buildings are all located in central Jakarta (Jakarta Pusat).
- Historic Kota Tua (Old Town), Sunda Kelapa port, and seafood markets are all located in North Jakarta (Jakarta Utara).
- Jakarta Selatan, or South Jakarta: upscale shopping, trendy cafés, and hangouts for expats.
- Dutch colonial architecture and Chinatown (Glodok) are features of West Jakarta (Jakarta Barat).

Travel Advice: The traffic in Jakarta is legendary—and not in a good way. To avoid taxi scams, use ride-hailing apps like Grab and Gojek or the MRT (Mass Rapid Transit) on important routes. Ojeks, or motorbike taxis, are the quickest choice for short trips.

2.2 Highlights of History and Culture

The history of Jakarta is a synthesis of international trade, colonial influence, and indigenous legacy.

- The city's Dutch colonial core, Kota Tua (Old Town), is home to the Jakarta History Museum, quaint cafés like Café Batavia, and cobblestone streets. See the historic structures at dusk as the light turns golden.
- See the handloading of classic wooden schooners (phinisi) at Sunda Kelapa Harbor, a live reminder of Indonesia's maritime heritage.
- Mounted at 132 meters, the National Monument (Monas) provides sweeping views from its

observation platform. In order to avoid lines, arrive early.

- Indonesia's religious tolerance is symbolized by the Jakarta Cathedral and Istiqlal Mosque, which are located across from one another. The largest mosque in Southeast Asia is called Istiqlal.

- Taman Mini Indonesia Indah is a cultural park that offers a brief overview of Indonesia's variety by displaying traditional homes, clothes, and dances from its several provinces.

Insider Tip: To avoid the midday heat and tour bus throngs, Kota Tua is best visited early in the morning or late in the afternoon.

2.3 Adventures in Cooking

Jakarta's culinary culture is a microcosm of Indonesia; it is bold, spicy, and incredibly diverse.

Must-Try Recipes:

- Nasi Uduk is coconut milk rice accompanied by crispy shallots, sambal, and fried chicken.
- Soto Betawi, a Jakartan dish, is a rich beef soup made with coconut milk, potatoes, and herbs.
- Kerak Telor is a type of street-side omelette made with dried shrimp, coconut, and sticky rice.
- Locals adore Bakso, a flavorful meatball soup.
- Martabak is a savory or sweet stuffed pancake, and the chocolate-cheese variety is particularly delicious.

Food Districts to Investigate:

- For Chinese-Indonesian fusion cuisine, visit Glodok, Chinatown.
- Menteng: chic coffee shops and contemporary Indonesian food.
- Kelapa Gading is well-known for its variety of street food and night market.

Practical Tip: If street food is freshly prepared and served hot, it is safe to try. Always keep hand sanitizer and bottled water on hand.

2.4 Purchasing and Memorabilia

From obscure antique shops to mega-malls, Jakarta has plenty to offer every type of shopper.

- Grand Indonesia and Plaza Indonesia offer upscale dining options, luxury goods, and comfortable air conditioning.
- The largest textile market in Southeast Asia is Tanah Abang Market; haggle hard and arrive early.
- Vinyl records, old cameras, and batik fabrics can be found in the antique market on Jalan Surabaya.
- Pasar Baru: Inexpensive clothing, accessories, and shoes in a vintage arcade.

Ideas for souvenirs include hand-drawn batik, locally produced spices, silver jewelry, and Indonesian coffee (Java Arabica or Sumatra Mandheling).

2.5 Entertainment & Nightlife

With alternatives to suit every taste, Jakarta comes alive after dark.

- Live Music & Jazz Bars: For elegant evenings, visit The Prohibition or Motion Blue Jakarta.
- Rooftop Lounges: Come for sunset at SKYE Bar, which offers expansive views of the city skyline.
- Night Markets: Food vendors in Mangga Besar remain open till the wee hours of the morning.
- Cultural Shows: Traditional dance, theater, and music performances are held in Gedung Kesenian Jakarta.

Although pickpocketing can occur in crowded areas, Jakarta is generally safe. Use reliable transportation, stay in well-lit areas, and keep valuables safe.

Useful Travel Advice for Jakarta

- Climate: Always hot and muggy; dress in airy, light clothing.
- Language: Bahasa Indonesia is helpful in marketplaces and local regions, while English is used in hotels and tourist destinations.
- Money: Although there are many ATMs, stay away from those in remote or poorly lighted areas.
- Etiquette: When visiting places of worship, dress modestly and refrain from making public shows of affection.
- Connectivity: Local SIM cards provide more dependable connection, but free Wi-Fi is frequently available in cafés.

Jakarta will reward you with cultural delights, delectable food, and a crash course in the spirit of modern Indonesia, but it will also try your patience with its traffic and humidity. Skyscrapers next to colonial artifacts, food stalls next to upscale restaurants, and tradition thriving in the bustle of a megacity—the city provides an honest introduction to the contrasts that make Java so alluring, whether you are visiting for a day or several.

Now that you have Jakarta as your starting point, you will be prepared to explore Java's landscapes and customs in greater detail. We'll slow down and travel to Central Java in the following chapter, where ancient temples, royal palaces, and Javanese artwork narrate tales that predate the island's biggest volcano.

CHAPTER 3: CENTRAL JAVA - PALACES, TEMPLES, AND AGELESS CUSTOMS

The cultural center of the island is central Java, where communities continue centuries-old customs, royal palaces reverberate with Javanese grandeur, and ancient temples soar over foggy plains. This area offers more than just tourism; it's about experiencing a slower pace of life, sensing Java's spiritual energy, and taking in the creativity weaved into everything from gamelan music to batik fabrics. Central Java offers experiences that will linger in your memory long after you've left, whether you're following in the footsteps of monarchs or witnessing the sunrise over a natural beauty.

3.1 Important Cities & Regions

Jogja (Yogyakarta)

Yogyakarta, sometimes referred to as Java's cultural center, combines old world charm with modern innovation. It is the location of some of Indonesia's most recognizable landmarks, a flourishing art scene, and royal legacy. While adjoining Malioboro Street is teeming with markets, food vendors, and souvenir shops, the Kraton (Sultan's Palace) is still a bustling royal house.

Surakarta, alone

Solo, a less visited but no less culturally rich city than Yogyakarta, is renowned for its serene royal grounds, exquisite wayang kulit (shadow puppetry), and exquisite batik artistry.

The Magelang

The entrance to Borobudur Temple is in Magelang, a peaceful village north of Yogyakarta that is encircled by picturesque highlands and coffee fields.

3.2 renowned temples

Two of Southeast Asia's biggest monuments, UNESCO World Heritage sites, are located in central Java.

Temple of Borobudur

- The biggest Buddhist temple in the world, Borobudur was constructed in the ninth century and is a marvel of stupas and stone reliefs.
- The best time to visit is around daybreak, when the temple is glowing gold and the surrounding valleys are covered in mist.
- Useful Tip: Special tickets must be purchased in advance for sunrise tours. For the chilly early morning, pack a lightweight jacket.

Temple of Prambanan

- The Trimurti—Shiva, Vishnu, and Brahma—are honored at this complex of Hindu temples from the ninth century.

- Renowned for its intricate stone carvings and lofty, pointed architecture.
- An enchanted cultural event, evening Ramayana ballet performances are held against the illuminated temple backdrop.

Other Prominent Websites

- Candi Plaosan is a complex of twin temples that combines Hindu and Buddhist elements.
- Smaller temples with distinctive sculptures and history close to Borobudur are Candi Mendut and Pawon.

3.3 Cultural Heritage & Royal Palaces

The Kraton of Yogyakarta

This huge palace is a live representation of Javanese tradition rather than just a museum. Inside, you'll discover elaborately adorned pavilions, royal antiques, and daily cultural events including classical Javanese dance and gamelan orchestras.

A tiny but exquisitely preserved royal home, Pura Mangkunegaran (Solo) is renowned for its exquisite Javanese architecture and collections of ceremonial objects, traditional attire, and weapons.

Etiquette Tip: Wear modest clothing, covering your knees and shoulders, and abide by the laws about taking pictures in private or sacred spaces when you visit palaces.

3.4 Conventional Crafts and Arts

For craft enthusiasts, Central Java is a veritable gold mine.

- **Batik:** With their unique designs, Solo and Yogyakarta are major centers for batik. Take a workshop to learn the steps and attempt making your own item.

- **Wayang Kulit:** Epics like the Ramayana and Mahabharata are brought to life through shadow puppet shows. Even a brief performance provides an enchanted look into Javanese storytelling, and shows can go on for hours.
- **Gamelan Music:** Hypnotic tunes are produced by this orchestra of bronze instruments. You can go to free performances at cultural centers or the Kraton.

3.5 Outdoor Adventures & Natural Wonders

As inspiring as its cultural treasures are the landscapes of Central Java.

- **Mount Merapi:** One of the most active volcanoes in Indonesia, Merapi provides guided jeep trips across its lava fields and rocky slopes.

- The Dieng Plateau is a highland area with steaming craters, ancient temples covered in mist, and vibrant volcanic lakes. In order to avoid afternoon fog, it is best to visit early.
- **Selo Village:** A picturesque place to halt between Merapi and Mount Merbabu, ideal for walks in the countryside and photography.

Practical Tip: Employ certified guides for volcano treks because safety is the top concern and conditions might change quickly.

3.6 Gastronomic Adventures

The food of Central Java is renowned for being more aromatic and sweet than that of other areas.

Must-Try Recipes:

- Gudeg is a rice, chicken, and egg dish made with sweet jackfruit. The most famous meal in Yogyakarta.
- Bakpia Pathok are mung bean paste-filled, flaky pastries that are frequently taken home as mementos.
- Wedang Ronde: This dish, which combines warm ginger tea with sticky rice balls, is ideal for chilly nights in the highlands.
- Sate Klatak: On the outskirts of Yogyakarta, grilled goat skewers served with curry sauce and lightly seasoned with salt.

Where to Dine:

- Legendary gudeg in Jogja is Gudeg Yu Djum.
- Pasar Beringharjo: Traditional snacks and beverages at market stalls.
- Sate Klatak Pak Pong is well-known for its succulent skewers that are cooked over iron rods.

3.7 Useful Advice for Central Java Travel

- **Best time to visit:** The best time to visit is during the dry season (May to October), when temples and volcanoes can be clearly seen.

- **Transportation:** Yogyakarta, Solo, and Semarang are all connected by train. Hire a driver or go on trips to remote places.

- **Language:** Although most people speak Bahasa Indonesia, many craftspeople and rural residents may speak Javanese as their primary language.

- **Money:** In tiny towns, cash is king. Keep small denominations on hand for local restaurants and markets.

- **Cultural Sensitivity:** Javanese culture places a high importance on being courteous. To show this, smile when you welcome someone, give and receive with your right hand, and refrain from pointing your feet at people or holy items.

History, spirituality, and artistic expression all converge in Central Java in a way that seems ageless. You can sense the deeply ingrained customs that influence Javanese life by strolling through royal courtyards, standing among Borobudur's stupas at sunrise, or watching shadow puppets dance in lamplight.

This area is worth taking your time exploring, not just because of its well-known temples but also because of the innumerable opportunities to meet locals, craftspeople, and take in the scenery that truly captures the essence of the island.

We go eastward to East Java in the following chapter, where daring tourists might discover rocky mountains, smoldering craters, and undiscovered coastline treasures.

CHAPTER 4: EAST JAVA - SECRETS OF THE COAST, WATERFALLS, AND VOLCANOES

East Java is a region of striking contrasts, where peaceful beaches meet untamed volcanic strength and busy port cities give way to peaceful highland farms. From the turquoise lake of Mount Ijen to the smoking crater of Mount Bromo, this area is less visited than Central Java yet is home to some of Indonesia's most remarkable natural wonders. East Java provides exciting scenery, inspiring cultural experiences, and undiscovered areas that seem unspoiled by time for individuals who are looking for both adventure and authenticity.

4.1 Important Cities and Points of Entry

The Surabaya

The second-biggest city in Indonesia serves as a key entry point to East Java. Surabaya, sometimes referred to as the "City of Heroes," was crucial to Indonesia's independence. Although the city is frequently viewed as a transit hub, visitors are rewarded with colonial architecture, exciting street food options, and bustling marketplaces.

Malang

With its Dutch-era boulevards, colorful murals, and convenient access to volcanic vistas, Malang is a charming, cooler highland city encircled by tea plantations.

Banyuwangi

Banyuwangi, Java's easternmost city, serves as the starting point for climbs up Mount Ijen and ferry crossings to Bali.

4.2 Mount Bromo: A Legend

Mount Bromo, which is a part of the Bromo Tengger Semeru National Park, is a must-see when visiting East Java.

- Why Go: One of Indonesia's most famous tourist experiences is seeing the sunrise over Bromo's lunar-like sea of sand.
- How to Get There: From Cemoro Lawang village, Probolinggo, or Malang.
- The best experience is when you take a jeep to Penanjakan Viewpoint at three in the morning. Mount Bromo's immaculate cone is visible as the horizon gradually gets brighter, while Mount Semeru can be seen smoking in the distance.

- Useful tip: Wear warm clothing because it can be as low as 5°C (41°F) before dawn. For the dusty caldera trek, pack a scarf or mask.

Mount Semeru Trekking

The highest peak in Java for serious hikers is Semeru (3,676 m). Although the two-day hike is strenuous, it provides breathtaking vistas and a genuine sense of achievement.

4.3 The Blue Fire Phenomenon and Mount Ijen

Mount Ijen, which is close to Banyuwangi, is well-known for two things: the unusual blue flames produced by burning sulfur gas and its acidic turquoise crater lake.

- The Blue Fire Hike: Set out for a guided hike to see the flames before dawn, departing at midnight.
- Daytime Beauty: The milky-blue lake, surrounded by rocky rocks, emerges as the sun rises.
- Wear a suitable gas mask (guides give them) because sulfur fumes can be extremely strong. Sturdy shoes are necessary because of the steep and slick drop into the crater.

Cultural Note: Sulfur miners lift huge loads from the crater while working in incredibly difficult conditions. To show their support, many tourists decide to tip them or purchase tiny sulfur carvings as mementos.

4.4 Highland Escapes & Waterfalls

The volcanic landscape of East Java is dotted with stunning and revitalizing waterfalls.

Sewu Waterfall in Tumpak

- Often referred to as "Indonesia's Niagara Falls," this magnificent waterfall in Lumajang falls in an ideal semicircle.
- The best time to visit is in the morning, when the mist is illuminated by the sun for stunning photos.
- Wear shoes that can withstand water because the access entails a steep and slick slope.

The Madakaripura Waterfall

- Gajah Mada, the fabled prime minister of the Majapahit Empire, is supposed to have meditated at this holy location, which is close to Bromo.
- To get to the main falls, expect to trek across streams that are ankle deep.

Coban Pelangi and Coban Rondo

- More accessible and scenic, it's ideal for a leisurely day excursion from Malang.

4.5 Secrets of the Coast

East Java has some hidden treasures for those who are ready to go off the usual route, even though its beaches aren't as well-known as Bali's.

Island of Red (Pulau Merah)

- Renowned for its lengthy sandy beach and reddish soil. Gentle waves make it ideal for novice surfers.

G-Land's Plengkung Beach

- A top-notch surf spot that draws skilled surfers from all over the world. situated inside the National Park of Alas Purwo.

Papuma Pantai
- This Jember beach is a picturesque getaway with its white sand, turquoise waves, and striking rock formations.

Practical Tip: Only swim in approved safe zones because many of the beaches here have strong currents.

4.6 Festivals & Cultural Exchanges

Ponorogo Reog
During festivals and other special occasions, a spectacular traditional dance is performed, adorned with peacock feathers and lion masks.

A fun traditional play that blends comedy, music, and social commentary is presented by the **Ludruk Theatre in Surabaya.**

Mount Bromo's Yadnya Kasada Festival
To show their gratitude to the gods, the Tenggerese trek to Mount Bromo's crater in July and toss sacrifices of food, animals, and cash into the volcano. Visitors are welcome to watch, but they must show respect for this holy rite.

4.7 East Java's Culinary Highlights

Compared to Central Javan cuisine, East Javanese food is typically stronger and more spicy.

Must-Try Recipes:

- Rawon is a keluak-nut-flavored black beef soup that is typically served with salted egg and rice.

- Peanut sauce, roasted cow snout slices, and a tart fruit and vegetable salad are the ingredients of Rujak Cingur.
- Sego Tempong, a popular dish in Banyuwangi, is rice served with fried fish, veggies, and spicy sambal.
- Bakso Malang is a meatball soup that is ideal for chilly highland evenings. It contains tofu, fried dumplings, and noodles.

Foodie Tip: For a gastronomic excursion, visit Pasar Atom or G-Walk night market. Surabaya boasts one of Java's top street food scenes.

4.8 Useful Advice for East Java Travel

- For a clear sky, May through October is the ideal time to visit. For volcano treks, stay away from the January–February peak wet season.

- Transportation: Major cities are connected by train; but, if you want to see natural sights, you should hire a driver or take a tour.
- Health & Safety: Always confirm the activity status from official sources before visiting a volcano because eruptions can happen suddenly.
- Warm clothes, hiking boots, a rain jacket, sunscreen, and bug repellent are essential items to pack.
- Respect Local Customs: Wear modest clothing and get permission before taking pictures of individuals in traditional and rural locations.

A wilder, more daring side of the island may be found in East Java, where you can hike to hidden waterfalls by midday, stand on the rim of an active volcano before breakfast, and watch the sun set over a secluded beach in the evening. Curiosity and adaptability are rewarded in this area, where the most memorable events can result from unforeseen detours.

East Java will leave you with tales fit for an epic travel journal, whether you're chasing the glow of Bromo at dawn, inhaling the sulfur mist at Ijen, or just savoring a bowl of rawon at a roadside vendor.

We'll then go into West Java, which offers a mix of contemporary metropolitan life and Sundanese friendliness, as well as rolling tea plantations and volcanic hot springs.

CHAPTER 5: WEST JAVA - CITY LIFE, TEA, AND MOUNTAINS

West Java has a captivating fusion of urban energy, cultural diversity, and scenic beauty. Here, the bustle of Bandung's creative scene and the expansive metropolis of Jakarta combine with the verdant mountains and foggy tea farms of the highlands. The Sundanese people, who are noted for their friendly hospitality, beautiful language, and passion for the natural world, are from West Java. West Java offers experiences that are revitalizing and healing, whether you're looking for a weekend getaway from the city or a more in-depth investigation of the local customs.

5.1 Key Locations & How to Get There

Jakarta

The majority of foreign visitors enter Indonesia through Jakarta, the country's capital. Despite being frequently considered a stopover city, Jakarta boasts world-class shopping centers, a thriving food scene, and historic neighborhoods like Kota Tua (Old Town).

Bandung

Bandung, a cool-weather city surrounded by volcanic highlands, has been dubbed the "Paris of Java." It's a hub for creative design, outlet shopping, and café culture. It is a great starting point for day trips because of its close proximity to mountain resorts.

Bogor

Bogor, a short weekend escape for city people, is well-known for its botanical gardens and is situated just south of Jakarta.

5.2 Volcanic Landscapes & Highland Retreats

Tangkuban Perahu Volcano

- This stratovolcano, which is roughly 30 kilometers from Bandung, is associated with a local myth of forbidden love and looks like an "upturned boat."
- It is one of the most accessible volcanoes in Java since visitors may drive up to the crater rim.
- The best time to visit is in the morning, when the crater isn't yet covered in mist.

Highlands of Puncak

- Between Jakarta and Bandung, there is a picturesque mountain pass that is well-known for its endless tea plantations.
- Excellent for tea tasting at plantation homes, photography, and quick walks.

- Travel Tip: Steer clear of weekends if you can because city tourists might cause excessive traffic.

Mount Papandayan

- A geothermal marvel including sulfur lakes, Edelweiss meadows, and steamy fumaroles.
- More daring trekking experience, less crowded than Tangkuban Perahu.

5.3 Sundanese customs and cultural heritage

The Sundanese, who live in West Java, value music, respect, and a close relationship with nature.

Bandung's Saung Angklung Udjo

- A cultural center devoted to conserving the bamboo instrument known as the angklung, which has been recognized by UNESCO.
- Visitors can participate in interactive workshops, witness performances, and learn to play.

Naga Kampung

- A traditional town without electricity or contemporary amenities that preserves traditional Sundanese architecture and customs.
- A local guide who can explain the cultural importance of everyday living here is the best way to visit.

Golek Wayang

- A distinctive type of wooden puppet theater from the Sundanese that is frequently seen at cultural festivals.

5.4 Outdoor Adventures & Nature

Bogor Botanical Gardens

- More than 15,000 plant species, including rare orchids and enormous palms, may be found in these gardens, which were established in 1817.
- Ideal for a picnic or a leisurely stroll.

Putih Ciwidey & Kawah

- A cold alpine forest envelops a strange crater lake with milky turquoise water.
- Wearing a mask is advised because the sulfur-rich air can be rather powerful.

Ratu Pelabuhan

- Known for its fishing and surfing, this seaside hamlet has local legends about the Queen of the Southern Sea.

Cukang Taneuh, or Green Canyon

- A secret paradise with striking cliffs and green lakes. It is best explored by swimming via its little passageways or by small boat.

5.5 West Java's Culinary Highlights

Compared to other Indonesian cuisine, Sundanese food is typically less greasy and more herbal. Traditionally, sambal (chili paste) and lalapan (raw vegetables) accompany meals.

Must-Try Recipes:

- Nasi Timbel is a dish of rice wrapped in banana leaves and served with sambal, tofu, and fried chicken.
- Sayur Asem is a sweet-sour vegetable soup made with tamarind.

- Similar to gado-gado but without the cooking, karedok is a raw vegetable salad with peanut sauce.
- Batagor is a popular street dish in Bandung that consists of fried tofu and fish dumplings with peanut sauce.
- Colenak is grilled fermented cassava served with a sauce made of coconut sugar.

Where to Dine:

- Braga Street in Bandung is home to hip bistros and cafés.
- For a blend of contemporary and traditional cuisine, visit Floating Market Lembang.
- Bogor's street vendors selling satay and fresh tropical fruit.

5.6 Purchasing & Ingenious Discoveries

Bandung Factory Outlets

- The fashion hub of Indonesia is Bandung, which sells premium apparel at discount costs. Dago and Jalan Riau are well-liked locations.

The Pasar Baru Trade Center

- A huge shopping center featuring traditional clothing, fabrics, and batik.

The Cihampelas Walk

- Known as "Jeans Street," this pedestrian-friendly area has themed cafés and oddball stores.

5.7 Useful Advice for West Java Travel

- For outdoor activities, the dry season (May to September) is the ideal time to visit.

- Transportation: The trains that run between Bogor, Bandung, and Jakarta are pleasant and picturesque. Hire a private driver for mountainous places.
- Weather: Pack a light jacket because the highlands are cool. It can get hot and muggy along the coast.
- Cultural Etiquette: Sundanese people are courteous and soft-spoken; refrain from acting loudly or aggressively.
- Safety tip: Keep an eye on possessions at busy marketplaces in cities. Dress modestly and honor local traditions when you're in a rural location.

West Java is a location of equilibrium, with neighboring highlands providing peaceful havens and vibrant, creative towns. You can enjoy tea in a plantation house in the morning, go shopping for modern clothing in the afternoon, and watch the sunset over a crater lake as the day comes to a close.

Every bend in the road offers a new view worth stopping for, Sundanese hospitality makes even strangers feel like family, and modern life coexists peacefully with tradition.

The road will lead you toward Jakarta's colorful turmoil and the starting point for other excursions outside of Java as you leave behind the foggy hills and bustling streets of West Java.

CHAPTER 6: JAKARTA - THE VITALITY AND CONTRASTS OF THE CAPITAL

Jakarta is a real, breathing entity that requires you to feel its pulse; it is not a city you "pass through." Beneath the blaring traffic and neon-lit shopping centers, the Indonesian capital is a large, turbulent, and unrelenting city that offers an intriguing fusion of opportunity, culture, and history. Jakarta offers layers to visitors who approach it patiently and with interest, from world-class museums and colonial-era architecture to exciting nightlife and street food experiences. This metropolis unites all of Indonesia, resulting in a cultural melting pot that is unmatched throughout the archipelago.

6.1 Recognizing the Character and Layout of Jakarta

Each of the municipalities that make up Jakarta—Central, North, South, East, and West—has a distinct personality.

- **Central Jakarta** Merdeka Square, the National Monument (Monas), and important government buildings can be found in this political and historical center.
- **North Jakarta** is a coastal region that includes the ancient Kota Tua, the port of Sunda Kelapa, and restaurants serving seafood.
- **South Jakarta:** The fashionable and affluent area, featuring shopping centers, pubs, and embassies.
- **West Jakarta** is the location of traditional marketplaces and Chinatown (Glodok).
- **East Jakarta:** More residential area with lots of greenery and cultural parks.

Travel Tip: Because of Jakarta's notoriously bad traffic, stay away from rush hours (7–9 AM, 5–8 PM) and, for convenience, use ride-hailing apps like Grab or Gojek.

6.2 Cultural Highlights & Historical Landmarks

Old Town Kota Tua

- Jakarta started out as Batavia, a Dutch colonial city.
- Explore the Jakarta History Museum, take a stroll in Fatahillah Square, and have coffee at the colonial-era jewel Café Batavia.
- Renting vintage bicycles and seeing street entertainers to the allure.

Monas National Monument

- The most recognizable landmark in Jakarta, representing the nation's independence.
- There are expansive views of the metropolitan skyline from the viewing deck.
- The history of Indonesia's fight for independence is told in the museum within.

Mosque of Istiqlal and Cathedral of Jakarta

- These locations, which are across from one another, represent Indonesian religious peace.
- The cathedral is a neo-gothic architectural gem, while Istiqlal is the biggest mosque in Southeast Asia.

6.3 Time-Well Spent at Museums

Although many tourists overlook Jakarta's museums, they are crucial to comprehending the identity of the country.

- Ancient Hindu-Buddhist treasures, ethnic costumes, and prehistoric items are all on display at the National Museum.

- Housed in a beautifully restored edifice, Museum Bank Indonesia offers an unexpectedly captivating look at the country's economic history.

- The Wayang Museum features a collection from all across Asia and is devoted to Indonesia's traditional puppet arts.

- The MACAN Museum is a modern art gallery that features both foreign and contemporary Indonesian artwork.

Insider Tip: Schedule your trips appropriately because many museums are closed on Mondays.

6.4 Waterfront Retreats & Urban Green Spaces

- Menteng's tranquil Taman Suropati Park is a great place for morning strolls and local artistic events.
- Jakarta's primary recreation center, Ancol Dreamland, features an aquarium, an amusement park, and a beach.
- Kepulauan Seribu, or the Thousand Islands: These islands provide a short tropical getaway without leaving the province and are reachable by boat from Marina Ancol.

6.5 Shopping: From High-End Malls to Street Markets

The commercial environment in Jakarta reflects the diversity of its populace.

Regarding Conventional Discoveries:

- Pasar Baru is a historic marketplace including traditional foods, batik, and textiles.
- Glodok Chinatown is well-known for its Chinese-Indonesian cuisine, kitchenware, and herbs.

For Luxury & Modern Fashion:

- Grand Indonesia and Plaza Indonesia are upscale shopping centers including gourmet restaurants, art exhibits, and global brands.
- Blok M: A blend of street food, neighborhood stores, and reasonably priced clothing.

6.6 Jakarta's Culinary Adventures

Jakarta's culinary culture incorporates cuisines from all throughout the archipelago, reflecting the city's cultural variety.

Classics of Street Food:

- Nasi Uduk Betawi consists of coconut rice, tempeh, sambal, and fried chicken.
- Jakartan-only kerak telor is a spicy omelet made with sticky rice.
- A creamy beef soup made with coconut milk and flavorful spices is called soto betawi.

Best Dining Experiences:

- Lara Djonggrang is a charming eatery that offers cuisine from all across Indonesia.
- In a colonial home, Bunga Rampai offers sophisticated historical dining.

- Menteng Hawker Stalls: For regional delicacies and late-night nibbles.

Practical Tip: Steer clear of prepared foods that have been left out; freshly cooked and served hot street food is usually safe.

6.7 Cultural Events and Nightlife

With a variety of rooftop lounges, live music venues, and cultural events, Jakarta comes alive after sunset.

- SKYE Bar is a rooftop bar offering breathtaking views of the city skyline.
- Once a popular destination for backpackers, Jalan Jaksa today has a variety of laid-back pubs and cafés.
- Taman Ismail Marzuki is a cultural hub for festivals of dance, theater, and cinema.

6.8 Useful Travel Advice for Jakarta

- In order to prevent floods, the dry season (May to September) is the ideal time to visit.

- **Transportation:** MRT and TransJakarta buses are affordable and dependable, while ride-hailing applications offer the quickest route.

- **Safety:** Keep valuables close at hand because pickpocketing can occur in busy settings.

- **Language:** Most people speak Bahasa Indonesia; English is spoken mostly in tourist areas but not much elsewhere.

- **Dress Code:** Modern and urban, however modest attire is acceptable at places of worship.

Jakarta is a paradox: chaotic and cultured, taxing and invigorating. It's a city that rewards the traveler who looks farther rather than giving away its beauty at first sight. Jakarta epitomizes Indonesia's diversity and aspirations, from the echoes of antiquity in Kota Tua to the modern glass towers of Sudirman, from the elegant high-end dining to the spicy scents of street-side sate.

Spend time here as a destination deserving of your schedule rather than just as a stopover. The pace of the capital may be quick, but if you pay attention, you'll find that the city captures the spirit and energy of the country.

CHAPTER 7: CENTRAL JAVA - MONUMENTS, CUSTOMS, AND EVERLASTING SCENERIES

The island's spiritual and cultural center is central Java, where tranquil rice terraces give way to rich volcanic slopes, traditional arts flourish in busy cities, and ancient temples rise from foggy plains. Here, life moves more slowly, history seems more real, and Javanese friendliness is at its most radiant. Travelers are rewarded with both grandeur and intimacy in Central Java, whether they are following in the footsteps of Buddhist pilgrims at Borobudur, admiring Hindu epics carved in stone at Prambanan, or enjoying tea in a mountain town.

7.1 The pulsating cultural center of Yogyakarta

Despite being administratively distinct from the province of Central Java, Yogyakarta, also known as "Jogja," serves as both its cultural hub and the entry point to the majority of the area's attractions.

Reasons to Go:

- It's the ideal starting point for seeing Prambanan and Borobudur.
- Gamelan music, wayang kulit (shadow puppetry), and batik are all still practiced there.

Things You Must See in Yogyakarta:

- The Sultan's palace at Kraton Yogyakarta serves as both a royal residence and a cultural museum, hosting daily Javanese art performances.
- Taman Sari Water Castle — A fanciful old royal garden and bathing complex.

- The city's primary shopping avenue for batik, silver jewelry, and regional delicacies is Malioboro Street.

Insider Tip: For convenient access to dining options, art galleries, and tour companies, book a room at a boutique hotel in Prawirotaman.

7.2 The Buddhist Wonder, Borobudur

One of Southeast Asia's greatest archaeological treasures is Borobudur, the world's largest Buddhist temple. It was constructed in the ninth century and is designed to mirror the Buddhist road to enlightenment.

Useful Information:

- Getting There: It takes around 1.5 hours to get there by automobile from Yogyakarta, about 40 km northwest.

- Best Time: With mist floating over the Kedu Plain and Mount Merapi in the distance, sunrise visits are enchanted.

- Visitors are given sarongs; modest attire is required.

Travel Tip: Schedule a guided tour. By narrating the stories the temple's reliefs portray, local guides help visitors understand them.

7.3 A Hindu Masterwork: Prambanan

Whereas Prambanan displays Hindu devotion, Borobudur honors Buddhism. Constructed around the same time period, this UNESCO World Heritage monument is made up of tall spires honoring Shiva, Vishnu, and Brahma.

Highlights:

- The tallest and most elaborate temple is Candi Shiva Mahadeva.
- During the dry season, Ramayana Ballet is performed outdoors with Prambanan as the backdrop.
- Nearby Temples: Take a tour of the charming but tiny Candi Sewu and Candi Plaosan temples.

Useful Advice: For golden-hour photography and reduced people, go in the late afternoon.

7.4 The Mystical Highlands of Dieng Plateau

The Dieng Plateau, which is 2,000 meters above sea level, is home to historic Hindu temples, thermal vents, and volcanic lakes.

Best Experiences:

- Telaga Warna (Colored Lake) is well-known for its mineral-based color changes.
- Among Java's oldest Hindu temples is the Arjuna Temple Complex.
- One of Indonesia's most breathtaking sunrises may be seen from Sikunir Hill.

Insider Tip: Bring warm clothes because it can get very cold at night (below 10°C).

7.5 The Quieter Royal City: Surakarta (Solo)

Though it receives fewer visitors, Surakarta, sometimes known as Solo, is just as rich in tradition as Yogyakarta.

Reasons to Go:

- It is a center for traditional Javanese art.
- Kraton Kasunanan and Mangkunegaran Palace are its two royal residences.

Don't overlook:

- The biggest batik market in Central Java is called Pasar Klewer.
- Cultural centers routinely host Wayang Kulit performances.
- Triwindu Market is a veritable gold mine of antiques and oddities.

Advice: If you want to see Mount Lawu and the enigmatic Sukuh and Cetho temples, Solo is an excellent place to start.

7.6 A Gastronomic Adventure in Central Java

The food of Central Java has rich, slow-cooked flavors and is sweeter than that of other regions of Indonesia.

Must-Try Recipes:

- Young jackfruit stewed in coconut milk and palm sugar is the basis for the Yogyakarta specialty known as "gudeg."
- Nasi Liwet is a fragrant rice dish made with coconut milk that is frequently served with veggies and chicken.
- Made from rice flour and coconut milk, serabi solo are little pancakes that are frequently covered with chocolate or banana.

Street Food Tip: On cold evenings, wedang ronde, a sweet ginger drink served with glutinous rice balls, is a must-try local food in Yogyakarta and Solo night markets.

7.7 Nature & Adventure

Although itineraries are dominated by temples, Central Java's natural scenery is just as captivating.

- The most active volcano in Indonesia, Mount Merapi, offers guided jeep tours that take visitors through lava fields and eruption-affected towns.
- Around midday, Jomblang Cave, a vertical cavern in Gunungkidul, appears to be filled with a mystical "light from heaven."
- Beach Escapes: Traditional horse cart rides and beautiful sunsets may be seen at south coast beaches like Parangtritis.

Safety Tip: Because situations can change quickly, only hike Mount Merapi or visit caverns with knowledgeable guides.

In addition to being a living museum, Central Java is a place where customs are alive and well, thriving and continuing to influence daily life. It's where adventurers are challenged by volcanic terrain, where the taste of gudeg remains long after the meal is finished, and where the spiritual energy of old temples meets the warm laughter of batik artisans.

Give Central Java more than a cursory look if you want to experience it fully. Stay long enough to sip tea while mist swirls around the mountains, listen to the gamelan reverberating through a peaceful courtyard, and watch the sunrise above Borobudur. By doing this, you will experience Central Java's soul as well as its sights.

CHAPTER 8: EAST JAVA - COASTAL WONDERS, WATERFALLS, AND VOLCANOES

The most striking area of the island is East Java, which has been shaped by wind, water, and fire. Here, gorgeous beaches run the length of the Indian Ocean and the Bali Strait, waterfalls plummet into green pools, and active volcanoes loom over agricultural valleys. Along with its rich cultural legacy, which includes historic temples and quaint fishing villages, it is a site of unadulterated natural beauty and adventure. East Java provides some of Indonesia's most remarkable travel experiences, whether you're hiking over the lunar-like caldera of Mount Bromo, admiring the blue crater lake of Ijen, or chasing waterfalls in verdant jungles.

8.1 East Java's gateway, Surabaya

Surabaya is more than just a transit hub because it is the provincial capital and the second-biggest city in Indonesia. This city features a distinctive fusion of contemporary business areas, colonial architecture, and multicultural heritage.

Principal Points of Interest:

- House of Sampoerna: An intriguing museum showing Indonesia's clove cigarette industry housed in a historic Dutch structure.
- Heroes Monument (Tugu Pahlawan): Honors Indonesia's fight for independence.
- The Arab Quarter and Chinatown are bustling with ancient mosques, temples, and marketplaces.

Useful Tip: The greatest place to begin a visit to Mount Bromo and Ijen is Surabaya. Before entering the countryside, many tourists take flights into Juanda International Airport.

8.2 Mount Bromo: Java's Icon

The main draw of East Java is Mount Bromo, an unearthly volcanic landscape located inside the enormous Tengger Caldera.

The Traditional Experience:

- Penanjakan Hill's Sunrise Viewpoint is the most well-known location to witness the sunrise over Mount Bromo, Mount Batok, and Mount Semeru in the distance.
- A huge expanse of volcanic ash that leads to Bromo's crater is known as the "Sea of Sand."
- Crater Rim Hiking: To get a glimpse of the steaming crater, ascend 253 steep stairs in a brief but strenuous hike.

Insider Tip: Select alternate vantage points like Seruni Point or King Kong Hill for less crowded views.

How to Get There:

- The majority of trips begin in the village of Cemoro Lawang.
- Accessible from Probolinggo via motorbike or jeep.

8.3 Mount Ijen: Emerald Lake and the Blue Fire

Two unique features of Mount Ijen are its surreal turquoise crater lake and the blue fire, which is a phenomenon that is only visible before sunrise and is created by burning sulfur fumes.

What to anticipate:

- In order to catch the blue fire before dawn, the night trek begins at midnight.

- Sulfur Miners: Take in the strenuous labor of miners who must lift large quantities of sulfur.
- The world's largest and most acidic lake, Crater Lake, is breathtaking in the dawn light.

Practical Advice: It's cold at night, so pack warm clothing and a suitable gas mask, which is typically supplied in guided tours. It's a moderately difficult hike.

8.4 Adventures in Waterfalls

East Java is home to some of Indonesia's most breathtaking waterfalls, many of which are concealed by verdant, tropical surroundings.

Essential Waterfalls to See:

- Known as "Indonesia's Niagara Falls," Tumpak Sewu is a stunning waterfall that tumbles over a semicircular rock.

- Madakaripura is a mysterious waterfall encircled by tall, mossy walls that is associated with the myth of the renowned Majapahit prime minister Gajah Mada.
- Coban Rondo & Coban Pelangi are family-friendly, easily accessible falls close to Malang.

Safety Tip: Wear strong shoes and be ready for several river crossings because trails might be slick.

8.5 Malang - The Center of Culture and Cuisine

Malang has a lively culinary scene, colonial-era streets, and a pleasant, relaxed vibe.

Highlights:

- Jodipan Colorful Village is a rainbow-painted attraction that was once a slum.

- Apple orchards, theme parks, and flower gardens may be found at the nearby resort region known as Batu Highlands.
- Sample Malang cuisine, including rawon (beef soup with black keluak nut) and bakso Malang (meatball soup).

Travel Tip: For those who would like to have a more laid-back city stay than Surabaya, Malang is an excellent starting point for Bromo tours and waterfall excursions.

8.6 Coastal Wonders & Beaches

The beach of East Java is just as striking as its mountains.

Top Selections:

- Near Jember is Papuma Beach, which features white sand and striking rock formations.

- Red Island Beach (Pulau Merah) is well-known for its breathtaking sunsets and surfing.
- One of the top surfing locations in Alas Purwo National Park is Plengkung Beach (G-Land).

Cultural Bonus: Traditional boat races are frequently held during fishing festivals in coastal areas.

8.7 Historical and Cultural Sites

East Java boasts a rich cultural legacy, but nature takes center stage.

- Trowulan is a Majapahit Empire archaeological site that features restored historic buildings, temples, and museums.
- Jawi Temple is a Hindu-Buddhist temple close to Pasuruan that dates back to the 13th century.
- Baluran National Park is referred to as "Little Africa" because of its fauna and savanna scenery.

Advice: To get the most out of your trip between cities, mix natural and cultural attractions.

8.8 Useful Advice for East Java Travel

- For trekking volcanoes and seeing unobstructed vistas, the dry season (May to October) is the ideal time to visit.
- Transportation: Since there is little public transportation, private vehicles or guided tours are advised.
- Accommodations range from luxurious resorts in Malang and Banyuwangi to modest guesthouses in remote regions.
- Health & Safety: Prior to visiting active sites, always review news of volcanic activity.

Towering volcanoes, roaring waterfalls, limitless beaches, and remnants of ancient history are all found in East Java. You may hike through verdant forests to discover hidden waterfalls by midday, stand on the edge of an active crater at dawn, and watch the sun set over the Indian Ocean in the evening.

East Java is genuinely remarkable not only for its natural beauty but also for the spirit of adventure it evokes. This is the Java of wild nature, breathtaking scenery, and friendly interactions in tiny towns. East Java offers travelers every kind of challenge and reward they could possibly want.

CHAPTER 9: TEA, FOOD, AND CULTURAL EVENTS

Java's streets celebrate and serve its essence on a dish.

In Java, food is more than simply sustenance; it's a legacy, a story, and a link between generations. Native foods, centuries of spice commerce, royal palace customs, and regional inventiveness are all woven together in each meal. In contrast, tea is more than just a drink; it's a custom, a break from the day, and a sign of welcome. Beyond the table, Java's squares and streets come alive with night markets, dances, and festivals, providing you with a unique glimpse of the island's vibrant culture.

This chapter will discuss the island's rich tea culture, where and how to dine like a local, and how to participate in both traditional and contemporary Javanese festivities.

9.1 Royal feasts, street food, and all in between

Street Food: The Daily Banquet

The street food scene in Java is a sensory assault, with the distinct smells of spices, bubbling woks, and sizzling grills. There are countless options, ranging from mobile kaki lima carts to modest warungs (family-run food booths).

- Yogyakarta's Gudeg A stew of young jackfruit cooked slowly with coconut milk and palm sugar. The local institution Gudeg Yu Djum is the best place to try it.
- Bakso is a meatball soup that is served with fried wontons, noodles, and tofu. Follow the locals as street vendors drive carts filled with enormous boiling pots.

- Sate Ayam: Thick peanut sauce accompanied by grilled chicken skewers. For a distinctive twist on the iron skewer, try Yogyakarta's Sate Klatak.
- Rice, blanched vegetables, and hot peanut sauce make up Nasi Pecel. popular for breakfast in East Java.

Insider Tip: The freshest food is typically found at the busiest stalls. Don't be afraid to ask vendors what they would advise newcomers to do.

Eating in Tradition with Royal Cuisine

Cooking was considered an art form in Javanese palaces, called keratons. Once reserved for the aristocratic, these recipes are now served in a few eateries.

- Nasi Liwet, a favorite of Solo's royal court, is aromatic rice made from coconut milk and served with chicken, tempeh, and eggs.

- Ayam Goreng Kalasan: Flavorful fried chicken marinated in spices and coconut milk. began in a village close to Yogyakarta.

Where to Go: Yogyakarta's Bale Raos serves food influenced by Sultan Hamengkubuwono's cuisine.

9.2 Teh Culture: From Tea Plantations to Warungs

When Dutch colonists established expansive estates in the highlands in the 1700s, Java's tea history began. Tea is ingrained in daily life nowadays.

Daily Tea Customs

- Locals drink hot teh tubruk, a potent, unfiltered tea made with entire leaves and lots of sugar, at warungs.

- Rock sugar is served with teh poci (tea in clay teapots) in Central Java, so you can adjust the sweetness of each cup to your preference.

Exploring Tea Plantations

- Kebun Teh Wonosari (Malang): Provides tastings, factory tours, and picturesque strolls across undulating tea fields.
- Picking tea leaves with local farmers is possible in the lesser-known Kalosari Tea Estate (Banyumas).

Insider Tip: The greatest time to visit a plantation is in the early morning, when workers are out gathering fresh leaves and the light is wonderful.

9.3 Festivals Every Year & How to Attend Them

Java's calendar is filled with deeply ingrained cultural festivals.

- Yogyakarta, Sekaten The Prophet Muhammad's birthday is celebrated for a week, complete with night markets, music, and the well-known Gamelan Sekaten performance.
- Grebeg Maulud (Surakarta): Royal processions in which masses of gunungan, or food, are distributed to the public as they parade through the streets.
- Tenggerese villagers ascend Mount Bromo to toss offerings into its crater during Yadnya Kasada (Bromo). A magnificent fusion of spectacle and commitment.
- Wayang Kulit All-Night Shows: Usually performed during religious or royal ceremonies, these shows feature puppet master (dalang) acts backed by gamelan music.

Traveler Tip: Always verify local calendars because festival dates vary annually and are based on the Islamic or Javanese lunar calendars.

9.4 Music, Dance, and Theater Performances

With each performance rich in symbolism and history, Java's arts are as delicious as its food.

- The illuminated Prambanan Temple serves as the backdrop for the spectacular outdoor performance of the ancient epic known as the Ramayana Ballet (Prambanan).
- Wayang Orang is a type of wayang theater that is performed live by actors dressed in ornate costumes.
- Gamelan concerts include hypnotic rhythms produced by metallic percussion ensembles.

Weekly public performances are offered by certain keratons.

Where to See It:

- Yogyakarta's Purawisata hosts nightly Ramayana Ballet performances that include supper packages.
- An important venue for traditional performances is Solo's Sriwedari Theatre.

9.5 You'll Love Cooking Classes & Night Bazaars

Bazaars at Night

Java's streets become a riot of flavor and light as the sun sets.

- Yogyakarta's Malioboro Street is crowded with food vendors, street entertainers, and gift shops.

- For late-night meals, the locals love Pasar Kembang (Surabaya).

Classes in Cooking

Cooking lessons are an intensive method to learn for tourists who wish to bring a bit of Java home.

- Using goods from the local market, ViaVia Yogyakarta teaches traditional dishes.
- West Javanese cuisine is the emphasis of the Java Private Culinary Class (Bandung), which is offered in small groups.

A market visit is a master class in ingredients and negotiating, so pick programs that involve it.

In Java, food, tea, and festivals are not discrete events; rather, they are woven into a rich cultural tapestry that beckons you to pause, sample, listen, and participate. You are participating in customs that have been treasured for centuries, whether you are watching dancers under the lights of a temple, drinking tea in a misty plantation, or standing at a street vendor with sambal on your lips.

You have to eat like the locals, drink like they drink, and rejoice like they celebrate if you want to get the complete Java experience. At that point, you cease being merely a guest and begin to become a part of the narrative.

CHAPTER 10: USEFUL ADVICE, SECURITY, AND CONSCIENTIOUS TRAVEL

Travel with assurance, decency, and sustainability.

Java is a rewarding and interesting place to visit, but as with any place, planning, awareness, and flexibility are necessary for a good trip. This chapter gives you the skills you need to travel with confidence while also honoring and contributing to the communities you visit, from being aware of local customs to knowing how to manage situations. Java's people are just as magical as its scenery and culture, and by planning your trip carefully, you can make sure that the appropriate things will make your trip unforgettable.

10.1 Contacts for Health, Safety, and Emergencies in Each Region

Tips for General Health

- Vaccinations: Four to six weeks before your trip, check with a travel clinic. Tetanus, typhoid, and hepatitis A vaccinations may be advised.
- Food Safety: Eat at crowded, high-volume stands, stay away from tap water (use bottled or filtered), and peel your own fresh fruit.
- Mosquito Protection: Because Java has a tropical environment, use insect repellent and, in rural areas, think about installing mosquito nets.

Fundamentals of Safety

- Although small theft, such as pickpocketing or bag snatching, sometimes happen in busy marketplaces or on public transit, Java is generally safe.
- Don't flaunt pricey electronics or jewelry.

- Tell someone about your vacation plans if you plan to hike or explore off-the-beaten paths in rural or isolated locations.

Indonesian Emergency Numbers

- Officers: 110
- Fire and Ambulance: 118 or 119
- Look for marked posts in tourist locations; Yogyakarta/Bali Tourist Police are frequently more fluent in English.

Local Advice:

- **Jakarta:** Have local taxis or ride-hailing apps (Grab/Gojek) available for prompt transportation in an emergency because heavy traffic can delay emergency services.
- **East Java (volcanic hikes):** Prior to ascending Mount Bromo or Ijen, review reports on seismic activity.

- **Central Java:** Keep your valuables safe and be aware of your escape routes because processions and festivals can result in crowded areas.

10.2 How to Stay in Touch - Travel Apps & SIM Cards

SIM cards

Although speeds may differ, Indonesia's mobile network coverage is surprisingly wide, even in rural Java.

- The best providers for travelers are Indosat (cost-effective for cities), XL Axiata (excellent price-service ratio), and Telkomsel (best coverage in rural areas).
- Where to Buy: Convenience stores like Indomaret/Alfamart, large malls, and airports all have official provider kiosks.
- Registration: SIM cards are legally required to be registered in your name, therefore bring your passport.

Apps for Travel That Have an Impact

- Maps & Navigation: Maps.me for hiking paths and Google Maps (offline mode).
- Transportation: Gojek and Grab for food delivery, automobile trips, and motorbike taxis.
- Translation: Download offline packs for Google Translate, which performs effectively in Indonesian.
- Payment methods: Some warungs and night markets now accept the well-known e-wallets GoPay, OVO, and Dana.

10.3 Money Advice — Electronic Payments, Currency Exchanges, and ATMs

Money and Exchange

- The Indonesian Rupiah (IDR) is used as the local currency. The notes are worth between 1,000 and 100,000 IDR.
- Airport exchanges frequently provide cheaper rates; use city exchange offices or ATMs for greater bargains, and just change enough for transportation.

Using an ATM

- Accessible in malls, cities, and even tiny towns.
- Minimize carrying too much cash at once, but withdraw bigger amounts to minimize penalties for recurring transactions.
- Avoid freestanding ATMs in remote locations; ATMs connected to banks are safer.

E-Payments Cashless payments are rapidly becoming the norm in Indonesia.

From cafes to cabs, QRIS (QR Code Indonesian Standard) is widely recognized in urban areas.

- In rural places where digital payments are uncommon, keep some cash on hand.
- Sustainable Travel: Supporting Local Communities

10.4 Sustainable tourism: giving back to local communities

Travelers that respect the environment and local customs are better able to preserve Java's beauty and culture.

Tips for Conscientious Travel

- Support local businesses by booking community guides, dining at family-run warungs, and booking accommodations that are owned by locals.
- Minimize Waste: Bring a reusable water bottle; tourist destinations are starting to include refill stations.

- Respect Wildlife: Steer clear of animal-exploitation attractions (such as performances featuring captive dolphins).
- Cultural Sensitivity: Wear a sarong when visiting temples; dress modestly in villages and other places of worship.

Giving Back & Volunteering

- Take part in beach cleanups along the coast.
- Participate in cultural workshops led by regional craftspeople to preserve customs.
- Think about homestays, where your money helps families directly.

10.5 Key Phrases in Indonesia to Make People Smile Locally

Knowing a few words in Bahasa Indonesia not only facilitates travel but also makes people feel better.

English	Indonesia	Pronunciation
Hello	Halo	HAH-lo
Good morning	Selamat pagi	suh-LAH-maht PAH-gee
Thank you	Terima Kasih	tuh-REE-mah KAH-see
How much?	Berapa?	buh-RAH-pah
Delicious?	Enak sekali!	EH-nahk suh-KAH-lee
Yes	Ya	yah
No	Tidak	TEE-dahk
Excuse me/Sorry	Maaf	MAH-ahf
Please	Tolong	TOH-long
Goodbye	Selamat	suh-LAH-maht

	tinggal	TING-gahl

Pro Tip: Because Indonesians value tourists who try, even a simple grin and terima kasih can transform a transaction into a cordial conversation.

Java rewards the well-prepared traveler with deeper, more meaningful experiences in addition to fewer travel difficulties. In addition to protecting yourself, you can also help the island's wellbeing by practicing sustainable tourism, keeping in touch, managing your finances sensibly, and taking safety seriously. When you combine these useful abilities with a few local expressions, doors will literally and symbolically open up to experiences that are above the average tourist excursion.

Responsible travel in Java is ultimately about respect—for the people, the places, and the stories you become a part of—rather than following laws.

Printed in Dunstable, United Kingdom

74216392R00067